متن
الأربعين النووية
للإمام النووي

An-Nawawi's
FORTY HADITH

Second Edition: December 2003

Supervised by:

ABDUL MALIK MUJAHID

E-mail:darussalam@naseej.com.sa
Headoffice
Tel: 00966-4033962, 4043432 Fax: 00966-4021659
E-mail: darussalam@awalnet.sa
Website: http://www.dar-us-salam.com.

OUR BRANCHES, AGENTS AND STOCKISTS

Riyadh

Olyah branch	: Tel: 00966-1-4614483	Fax: 4644945
Malaz branch	: Tel: 00966-1-4735220	Fax: 4735221
Jeddah	: Tel: 00966-2-6879254	Fax:6336270
Al-Khobar	: Tel:00966-3-8692900	Fax: 00966-3-8691551
U.A.E	: Tel:00971-6-5632623	Fax: 5632624
Pakistan	: Tel:0092-42-724 0024	Fax: 7354072
U.S.A. Houston	: Tel:001-713-722 0419	Fax: 001-713-722 0431
New York	: Tel:001-718-625 5925	
U.K London	: Tel:0044-208 520 2666	Mobile: 0044-794 730 6706
		Fax: 0044-208 521 7645

متن
الأربعين النووية
للإمام النووي

An-Nawawi's
FORTY HADITH

DARUSSALAM
GLOBAL LEADER IN ISLAMIC BOOKS
Riyadh • Jeddah • Al-Khobar • Sharjah
Lahore • London • Houston • New York

© Maktaba Dar-us-Salam, 1996

King Fahd National Library Cataloging-in-Publication Data

Maktaba Darussalam

An-Nawai's Forty Hadith-Riyadh.

144p., 8x12 cm.

ISBN 9960-740-27-7

1-Al-Hadith   I-Title

237.7 dc.   2031 / 14

Legal Deposit no. 2031/14
ISBN 9960-740-27-7

إنما الأعمال بالنيات

١ - عن أمير المُـؤْمنِينَ أبي
حَفصٍ عُمَرَ بن الخطاب رضي الله
عنه قال: سمعْتُ رَسولَ الله ﷺ
يقولُ: «إنَّما الأعْمَالُ بالنَّيَات وإنَّما
لِكُلِّ امْرِىءٍ ما نَوَى. فَمَنْ كانَتْ
هِجْرَتُهُ إلى الله ورسولِهِ فَهِجْرَتُهُ إلى

DEEDS DEPEND UPON INTENTIONS

1. On the authority of the Chief of the believers, Abû Hafs 'Umar ibn al-Khattâb رضى الله عنه who said: I heard the Messenger of Allah صلى الله عليه وسلم saying:

The rewards of deeds depend upon the intentions[1] and every person will get the reward according to what he has intended. Thus he whose

---

[1] Intention is determining in the heart upon some action. It is not right to utter orally any prescribed word or sentence for performing the worship.

الله ورَسُولِهِ، ومَنْ كانَتْ هِجْرَتهُ لِدُنْيا يُصِيبُها أو امْرَأَةٍ يَنْكِحُها فَهِجْرَتُهُ إلى ما هَاجَرَ إليه» رواهُ إماما المُحَدِّثِين أبُو عَبْدِ الله محمَّدُ بنُ إسْماعِيلَ بنِ إبْراهِيمَ بنِ المُغِيرَة بن بَرْدِزْبَةَ الْبُخارِيُّ وأبُو الْحُسَيْنِ مُسْلِمُ بنُ الحَجَّاجِ بنِ مُسْلِمٍ القُشَيْرِيُّ النَّيسَابُورِيُّ في صَحِيحَيْهِما اللَّذَيْنِ هُمَا أصَحُّ الْكُتُبِ الْمُصَنَّفَة.

migration was for Allah and His Messenger, his migration was for Allah and His Messenger, and he whose migration was to achieve some worldly benefit or to take some woman in marriage, his migration was for that for which he migrated.

It was related by the two *Imâms* of the scholars of *Hadith*, Abû 'Abdullah Muhammad ibn Ismâ'îl ibn Ibrâhîm ibn al-Mughîra ibn Bardizbah al-Bukhârî and Abû al-Husain Muslim ibn al-Hajjâj ibn Muslim al-Qushairî an-Naisâbûrî, in their two *Sahîhs*, which are more sound of the compiled books.

بيان الإسلام والإيمان والإحسان

٢ ـ عَنْ عُمَــرَ رضي الله عنه أيضاً قال: «بَيْنَمَا نَحْنُ جُلُوسٌ عِنْدَ رسُــولِ الله ﷺ ذَاتَ يَوْمٍ إِذْ طَلَعَ علينــا رَجُلٌ شَدِيدُ بَياضِ الثِّيابِ شَدِيدُ سَوَادِ الشَّعْرِ، لا يُرى عليه أَثرُ السَّفَرِ، ولا يَعْرِفُهُ مِنَّا أَحَدٌ، حتى جلَسَ إلى النبيِّ ﷺ فأَسْنَدَ رُكْبَتيْهِ

EXPLANATION OF ISLAM
IMAN AND *IHSAN*

2. Also on the authority of 'Umar رضى الله عنه who said:

One day while we were sitting with the Messenger of Allah صلى الله عليه وسلم, there appeared before us a man whose clothes were exceedingly white and whose hair was exceedingly black; no signs of journeying were to be seen on him and none of us knew him. He walked up and sat down by the Prophet صلى الله عليه وسلم resting his knees against his and

إلى رُكْبَتَيْهِ، ووَضَـعَ كَفَّيْهِ على فَخِـذَيْهِ وقال: يا محمَّدُ، أَخْبِرْني عَنِ الإِسْلامِ . فقال رسول الله ﷺ: الإِسْلامُ أَنْ تَشْهَدَ أَنْ لا إله إلاَّ الله وأَنَّ محمَّـداً رسولُ الله . وتُقِيمَ الصَّـلاة . وتُؤْتِي الزَّكـاة . وتَصُومَ رَمَضانَ . وتَحُجَّ الْبَيتَ إن اسْتَطَعْتَ إليه سَبِيلاً قال: صَدَقْت . فَعَجِبْنا له

placing the palms of his hands on his thighs, then he said: O Muhammad, tell me about Islam. The Messenger of Allah صلى الله عليه وسلم said: Islam is to testify that there is no god to be worshipped but Allah and that Muhammad is the Messenger of Allah, to perform the prayers, to pay the *Zakât*[1] , to fast in Ramadân, and to make the pilgrimage to the House (Ka'ba in Makka) if you are able to do so. He said: You have spoken rightly, and we were amazed at

---

[1] It means compulsory charity to be levied on a man's wealth and distributed among the poors.

يسْـأله ويُصدّقُهُ قال : فأخْبِرْني عَن

الإيمـان قال : أنْ تُؤمـن بـاللـه .

ومـلائِكَتِـه . وكُتُبِه . ورُسُله . واليوْم

الآخِر . وتُؤمنَ بالقَدَر خَيْرِه وشَرِّه .

قال : صَدَقْتَ . قال : فأخْبِرْني عن

الإِحْسَانِ . قال : أنْ تَعْبُدَ الله كأنَّكَ

him asking him and saying that he had spoken rightly. He said: Then tell me about *îmân*[1]. He said: It is to believe in Allah, His angels, His books, His messengers, and the Last Day, and to believe in divine destiny (preordainment), both the good and the evil thereof. He said: You have spoken rightly. He said: Then tell me about *ihsân*[2].

---

[1] *Iman* is generally translated as faith or belief in Allah, but in Islamic term rendered with its six pillars as mentioned in the above tradition of the Prophet صلى الله عليه وسلم .

[2] *Ihsan* cannot rendered in a single word, as it includes the vast meanings of right =

تَرَاهُ، فَإِنْ لَمْ تَكُنْ تَرَاهُ فَإِنَّهُ يَرَاكَ.

قَالَ: فَأَخْبِرْنِي عَنِ السَّاعَةِ. قَالَ:

مَا الْمَسْؤُولُ عَنْهَا بِأَعْلَمَ مِنَ

السَّائِلِ. قَالَ: فَأَخْبِرْنِي عَنْ

أَمَارَاتِهَا. قَالَ: أَنْ تَلِدَ الْأَمَةُ رَبَّتَهَا،

He said: It is to worship Allah as though you are seeing Him, and while you see Him not yet truly He sees you. He said: Then tell me about the Hour (day of judgement). He said: The one questioned about it knows no better than the questioner. He said: Then tell me about its signs. He said: That the slave-girl will give

action, charity, sincerity etc. So it is rendered as the highest level of deeds and worship (perfection i.e. when you worship Allah or do deeds, consider yourself as if you see him and if you cannot achieve this feeling or attitude then you must bear in the mind that He sees you as mentioned in above *Hadith*.

وأنْ تَرَى الْحُفَاةَ الْعُرَاةَ الْعَالةَ رِعاءَ الشَّاءِ يَتَطَاوَلُونَ في الْبُنْيانِ. ثُمَّ انْطَلَقَ فَلَبِثْتُ مَلِيًّا، ثمَّ قال: يا عُمَرُ، أتَدْري مَن السَّائِلُ؟ قُلتُ: الله ورسُولُهُ أعلَمُ. قال: فإنَّهُ جِبْريلُ

birth to her mistress[1] and that you will see the barefooted, naked, destitute herdsmen competing in constructing lofty buildings. Then he took himself off and I stayed for a time. Then he (the Prophet صلى الله عليه وسلم) said: O 'Umar, do you know who the questioner was? I said: Allah and His Messenger know

---

[1] This phrase has more than one interpretation. Among those one is that slave-girl will give birth to sons and daughters who will become free and so be the masters of those who bore them. The other meaning is that a time will come when children will be so unobedient to their mothers that they will treat them like slave-girls.

أَتَاكُمْ يُعَلِّمُكُمْ دِينَكُمْ» رواهُ
مُسْلِمٌ.

أركان الاسلام

٣ ـ عن أبي عَبْدِ الرَّحمنِ ـ عبدِ
اللهِ بن عُمَرَ بن الخَطَّابِ ـ رضي
اللهُ عنهُمَا ـ قال: «سَمِعْتُ رسولَ
اللهِ ﷺ يقولُ: بُنِيَ الإسلامُ على
خَمْسٍ: شهادَةِ أنْ لا إلهَ إلَّا اللهُ
وأنَّ محمَّداً رسولُ اللهِ. وإقامِ

best. He said: It was Gabriel, who came to you to teach you your religion.

It was related by Muslim.

PILLARS OF ISLAM

3. On the authority of Abû 'Abd ar-Rahmân 'Abdullah, the son of 'Umar ibn al-Khattâb رضى الله عنهما who said: I heard the Messenger of Allah صلى الله عليه وسلم saying:

Islam is based on five [pillars]: testifying that there is no god worthy to be worshipped but Allah and that Muhammad is the Messenger of Allah, performing the prayers, paying

الصَّلَاةِ، وَإِيتَاءِ الزَّكَاةِ، وَحَجِّ البَيْتِ وَصَوْمِ رَمَضَانَ» رواهُ البُخَارِيُّ وَمُسْلِمٌ.

الأعمال بخواتيمها

٤ ـ عن أبي عبْدِ الرَّحمن عبدِ الله بن مسعودٍ رضي الله عنه قال: حدَّثَنَا رسولُ الله ﷺ وهُوَ الصَّادِقُ المَصْدُوقُ: «إن أحَدَكُمْ يُجْمَعُ خَلْقُهُ في بَطْنِ أمِّهِ أرْبَعِينَ يوماً

the *zakât,* making the pilgrimage to the House, and fasting in Ramadân.

It was related by al-Bukhârî and Muslim.

RESULT OF DEEDS DEPENDS ON ITS LAST

4. On the authority of Abû 'Abd ar-Rahmân 'Abdullah ibn Mas'ûd رضى الله عنه who said: The Messenger of Allah صلى الله عليه وسلم and he is truthful, the believed, narrated to us:

Verily the creation of each one of you is brought together in his mother's womb for forty days in the form of *nutfa* (mixed drop

نُطْفَةً ، ثُمَّ يَكُونُ عَلَقَةً مِثْلَ ذلك ، ثُمَّ يَكُونُ مُضْغَةً مِثْلَ ذلك ، ثُمَّ يُرْسَلُ اليه المَلَكُ فَيَنْفُخُ فيه الرُّوحَ ، ويُؤْمَرُ بِأَرْبَعِ كَلِمَاتٍ : بِكَتْبِ رِزْقِهِ ، وأَجَلِهِ ، وعَمَلِهِ ، وشَقِيٌّ أو سَعِيدٌ . فَوَاللهِ الَّذِي لا إله غَيْرُهُ إِنَّ أَحَدَكُمْ لَيَعْمَلُ بِعَمَلِ أَهْلِ الجَنَّةِ حتى ما يَكُونَ بَيْنَه وبَيْنَهَا إلا ذِرَاعٌ فَيَسْبِقُ عليه الْكِتَابُ فَيَعْمَلُ بِعَمَلِ أَهْلِ

of male and female sexual discharge) then he is a clot of blood for a like period, then a morsel of flesh for a like period, then there is sent to him the angel who blows the breath of life into him and who is commanded about four matters: to write down his means of livelihood, his life span, his actions, and whether good or bad. By Allah, other than Whom there is no god, verily one of you behaves like the people of Paradise until there is but an arm's length between him and it, and that which has been written overtakes him and so he behaves like the people of

النَّارِ فَيَدْخُلُهَا، وإنَّ أحَدَكُمْ لَيَعْمَلُ
بِعَمَلِ أهْلِ النَّارِ حتى ما يَكُونُ بَيْنَهُ
وبَيْنَهَا إلَّا ذِرَاعٌ فَيَسْبِقُ عليه الكِتَابُ
فَيَعْمَلُ بِعَمَلِ أهْلِ الجنَّةِ فَيَدْخُلُهَا»
رواه البخاريُّ ومُسْلِمٌ .

إبطال المنكرات والبدع

٥ ـ   عَنْ أمِّ المُؤمِنِينَ أمِّ عَبْدِ اللهِ
عائِشَةَ رضي الله عنها قالَتْ : قالَ

Hell-fire and thus he enters it; and one of you behaves like the people of Hell-fire until there is but an arm's length between him and it, and that which has been written overtakes him and so he behaves like the people of Paradise and thus he enters it.

It was related by al-Bukhârî and Muslim.

REMOVE THE INNOVATION

5. On the authority of the Mother of the *Momineen* (faithful people) Umm 'Abdullah 'A'isha رضى الله عنها who said: The Messenger of Allah صلى الله عليه وسلم said:

رسولُ الله ﷺ: «مَنْ أَحْدَثَ في أَمْرِنا هذا ما لَيْسَ منه فهوَ رَدٌّ» رواهُ البُخاريُّ ومُسْلِمٌ. وفي روايةٍ لِمُسلمٍ: «مَنْ عَمِلَ عَمَلًا لَيْسَ عليه أَمْرُنا فهوَ رَدٌّ».

الحلال بيّن والحرام بيّن

٦ ـ عَـنْ أبـي عَبْـدِ الله النُّعْمَانِ بن بَشيرٍ رضي الله عنهما قالَ: سَمِعْتُ رسولَ الله ﷺ يقولُ:

He who innovates something in this matter of ours that is not of it will have it rejected.

It was related by al-Bukhârî and Muslim. In one version by Muslim it reads:

He who does an act which is not (in agreement) with our matter will have it rejected.

LAWFUL AND UNLAWFUL THINGS ARE CLEARED

6. On the authority of Abû 'Abdullah an-Nu'mân, the son of Bashîr رضى الله عنهما who said: I heard

«إِنَّ الْحَلَالَ بَيِّنٌ، وإِنَّ الْحَرَامَ بَيِّنٌ، وبَيْنَهُمَا أُمُورٌ مُشْتَبِهَاتٌ لا يَعْلَمُهُنَّ كَثِيرٌ مِنَ النَّاسِ، فَمَنِ اتَّقَى الشُّبُهَاتِ فَقَدِ اسْتَبْرَأَ لِدِينِهِ وعِرْضِهِ، ومَنْ وَقَعَ فِي الشُّبُهَاتِ وَقَعَ فِي الْحَرَامِ، كالرَّاعِي يَرْعَى حَوْلَ الحِمَى يُوشِكُ أن يَرْتَعَ فِيهِ، أَلَا وإِنَّ لِكُلِّ مَلِكٍ حِمَىً، أَلَا وإِنَّ حِمَى اللهِ مَحَارِمُهُ أَلَا وإِن فِي

the Messenger of Allah صلى الله عليه وسلم saying:

Verily that is lawful is plain and that which is unlawful is plain and between the two of them are doubtful matters about which many people do not know. Thus he who avoids doubtful matters clears himself in regard to his religion and his honour, but he who falls into doubtful matters falls into that which is unlawful, like the shepherd who pastures around a sanctuary, may be he graze therein. Truly every king has a sanctuary, and truly Allah's sanctuary is His prohibitions. Verily in the body there is a

الجَسَدِ مُضْغَة إذا صَلَحَتْ صَلَحَ الجَسَدُ كلَّه. وإذا فَسَدت فَسَدَ الجسد كله: ألا وهي القَلْبُ» رواهُ البخاريُّ ومُسْلِمُ.

الدين النصيحة

٧ ـ عن أبي رُقَيَّةَ تَميمِ بنِ أوْسٍ الدَّاريِّ ـ رضي الله عنه ـ «أنَّ النَّبيَّ ﷺ قال: الدِّينُ النَّصِيحة. قُلْنَا: لِمَنْ؟ قالَ: لله،

morsel of flesh which, if it be right, all the body is right and which, if it be diseased, all of it is diseased. Truly it is the heart.

It was related by al-Bukhârî and Muslim.

RELIGION IS SINCERITY

7. On the authority of Abû Ruqayya Tamîm ibn Aus ad-Dârî رضى الله عنه that the Prophet صلى الله عليه وسلم said:

Religion is sincerity[1]. We said: To whom? He said: To Allah

---

[1] The Arabic word al-nasiha has a variety of meanings. Among those are: good doing, doing justice, sincerity etc.

ولِكِتَـابِـهِ، ولِـرَسُولِـهِ، ولأئـمة المُسْلِمِين، وعامّتِهِم» رواهُ مُسْلِمٌ.

حرمة المسلم

٨ ـ عـن ابـن عُمَـرَ رضي الله عنهمـا: «أنَّ رسُولَ الله ﷺ قال: أمِرْتُ أَنْ أقاتِلَ النَّاس حتى يَشْهَدُوا أنْ لا إِلَهَ إِلاَّ الله وأنَّ محمداً رسولُ

and His Book, and His Messenger, and to the leaders of the Muslims and their common people.

It was related by Muslim.

PROTECTION OF A MUSLIM

8. On the authority of Ibn 'Umar رضى الله عنهما that the Messenger of Allah صلى الله عليه وسلم said:

I have been ordered to fight against people until they testify that there is no god to be worshipped but Allah and that Muhammad is the Messenger of

اللهِ ، ويُقِيمُوا الصَّلاةَ ، ويُؤْتُوا الزَّكاةَ ، فإِذَا فَعَلُوا ذلك عَصَمُوا مِنِّي دِمَاءَهُمْ وأمْوَالَهُمْ إلا بِحَقِّ الإِسْلامِ ، وحِسَابُهُمْ على اللهِ تعالى» رواه البُخارِيُّ ومُسْلِمٌ .

التكليف بما يستطاع

٩ ـ عـن أبـي هُرَيْرَةَ عَبْدِ الرَّحمَن بن صَخرٍ ـ رضي الله عنه ـ قال : سَمِعْتُ رسولَ اللهِ ﷺ يَقُول :

Allah and until they perform the prayers and pay the *zakât,* and if they do so, they will have gained protection from me for their lives and property, unless (they do acts that are punishable) in accordance with Islam, and their reckoning will be with Allah, the Exalted.

It was related by al-Bukhari and Muslim.

ORDERS DEPEND ON ABILITY

9. On the authority of Abû Huraira Abd ar-Rahmân ibn Sakhr رضى الله عنه who said: I heard the Messenger of Allah صلى الله عليه وسلم saying:

«مَا نَهَيْتُكُمْ عنه فاجْتَنِبُوهُ، وما أَمَرْتُكُمْ به فأتُوا منه ما اسْتَطَعْتُمْ، فإنَّمَا أَهْلَكَ الَّذِينَ مِنْ قَبْلِكُمْ كَثْرَةُ مَسَائِلِهِمْ واخْتِلافُهُمْ على أَنْبِيائِهِمْ» رواهُ البُخَارِيُّ ومُسْلِمٌ.

الاقتصار على الحلال الطيب

١٠ ـ عن أبي هُرَيْرَةَ رضي الله عنه قال: «قال رسولُ الله ﷺ: إنَّ

What I have forbidden to you, avoid, and what I have ordered you [to do], do, as much of it as you can. It was only their excessive questioning and their disagreeing with their Prophets that those people who were before you destroyed .

It was related by al-Bukhârî and Muslim.

TO SEEK THE GOOD AND LAWFUL THINGS

10. On the authority of Abû Huraira رضى الله عنه who said: The Messenger of Allah صلى الله عليه وسلم said:

اللهَ تعالى طَيِّبٌ لا يَقْبَلُ إلاّ طَيِّباً، وإنَّ اللهَ أَمَرَ المؤمنينَ بمَا أَمَرَ به المُرْسَلينَ، فقالَ تعالى : ﴿يا أَيُّها الرُّسُلُ كُلُوا من الطيِّباتِ واعمَلُوا صالحاً﴾ وقال تعالى : ﴿يا أَيُّها الَّذين آمَنُوا كُلُوا مِنْ طَيِّباتِ ما رزَقْناكُمْ﴾ ثُمَّ ذَكَرَ الرَّجُلَ يُطيلُ السَّفَرَ أَشْعَثَ

Allah, the Exalted is good and accepts only that which is good. Allah has commanded the believers to do that which He commanded the Messengers, and the Exalted has said: "O (you) Messenger! Eat of the lawful things, and do righteous deeds[1] ." And Allah, the Exalted has said: "O you who believe! Eat of the lawful things wherewith We have provided you[2] ." Then he mentioned [the case of] a man who, having journeyed far, is dishevelled and dusty and who spreads out

---

[1] al-Mu'minûn, 51.
[2] al-Baqarah, 172.

أغْبَرَ، يَمُدُّ يَدَيْهِ الى السَّماءِ يا رَبُّ يا رَبُّ، ومَطْعَمُهُ حَرَامٌ، ومَشْرَبُهُ حَرَامٌ، ومَلْبَسُهُ حَرَامٌ، وغُذِيَ بالحَرَامِ، فأنَّى يُسْتَجَابُ لهُ» رواهُ مُسْلِمٌ.

التورع عن الشبهات

١١ ـ عـن أبـي محمـدٍ الحَسَنِ بنِ عَلِيِّ بنِ أبي طالبٍ ـ

his hands to the sky [saying]: O *Rubb*[1]! O *Rubb*! — while his food is unlawful, his drink is unlawful, his clothing unlawful, and he is nourished unlawfully, so how can his invocation be accepted.

It was related by Muslim.

LEAVING THE DOUBTFUL THINGS

11. On the authority of Abû Muhammad al-Hasan, the son of

---

[1] *Rubb* means among other meanings, the Creator, the Sustainer, the Owner, the Provider and the One in Whose Hands is the disposal of all affairs.

سِبْطِ رسولِ اللهِ ﷺ وريحانته ـ

رضي الله عنهُما ـ قال: حفظتُ مِنْ

رسولِ اللهِ ﷺ « دَعْ ما يَريبُك الى

ما لا يَريبُك» رَوَاهُ الـتِّـرمِـذِيُّ

والنِّسائِي، وقال الترمذيُّ: حديثٌ

حسنٌ صَحيحٌ.

ترك ما لا يعني المسلم

١٢ ـ عن أبي هُرَيْرَةَ رضي الله

'Alî ibn Abî Tâlib, the grandson of the Messenger of Allah صلى الله عليه وسلم and the one much beloved of him رضى الله عنهما who said:

I memorised from the Messenger of Allah صلى الله عليه وسلم:

Leave that, which makes you doubtful for that, which does not make you doubtful.

It was related by at-Tirmidhî and an-Nasâ'î. At-Tirmidhî stated it as a *Hasan* (fair) and *Sahih* (sound) *Hadith*.

LEAVING THE UNCONCERNED THINGS

12. On the authority of Abû Huraira رضى الله عنه who said: the

عنه، قال: قالَ رسُولَ الله ﷺ «منْ حُسْنِ إسْلَامِ الْمَرءِ تَرْكُهُ ما لا يَعْنيه» حديثٌ حَسَنٌ رواهُ الترمذيُّ وغيرُهُ هَكَذا.

كمال الإيمان

١٣ ــ عن أبي حَمْـزَةَ أَنَس بن مالكٍ رضي الله عنه ـ خادمِ رسولِ الله ﷺ ـ عن النَّبيِّ ﷺ قال:

Messenger of Allah صلى الله عليه وسلم
said:

Part of someone's being a good
Muslim is his leaving alone that
which does not concern him.

A *Hasan* (fair) *Hadith* which was
related by at-Tirmidhî and others
in this form.

PERFECTNESS OF FAITH

13. On the authority of Abû
Hamza Anas ibn Mâlik رضي الله عنه ,
the servant of the Messenger of
Allah صلى الله عليه وسلم that the
Prophet صلى الله عليه وسلم said:

«لا يُؤْمِنُ أَحَدُكُمْ حتى يُحِبَّ لأخِيهِ ما يُحِبُّ لِنَفْسِهِ» رواهُ البُخارِيُّ ومُسْلِمٌ.

حرمة دم المسلم وأسباب إهداره

١٤ ـ عَنْ ابن مسعودٍ رضي الله عنه قال: قال رسولُ اللهِ ﷺ: «لا يَحِلُّ دَمُ امْرِىءٍ مُسْلِمٍ إلَّا بإحْدَى ثلاثٍ: الثَّيِّبُ الـزَّانِي، والنَّفْسُ

None of you [truly] be a believer until he wishes for his brother what he wishes for himself.

It was related by al-Bukhârî and Muslim.

PROTECTION OF MUSLIM'S BLOOD AND ITS SPLITTING

14. On the authority of Ibn Mas'ûd رضى الله عنه who said: The Messenger of Allah صلى الله عليه وسلم said:

The blood of a Muslim may not be splitted other than in one of the three (instances): the married person who commits adultery; a life for a life; and the

بِالنَّفْسِ ، وَالتَّارِكُ لِدِينِهِ ، المُفَارِقُ لِلْجَمَاعَةِ» رواهُ البُخَارِيُّ ومُسْلِمٌ .

آداب إسلامية

١٥ ـ عَنْ أَبِي هُرَيْرَةَ رضي الله عنه : أَنَّ رَسُولَ اللهِ ﷺ قال : «مَنْ كَانَ يُؤمِنُ بِاللهِ وَالْيَوْمِ الآخِرِ فَلْيَقُلْ خَيْراً أَوْ لِيَصْمُتْ، وَمَنْ كَانَ يُؤمِنُ بِاللهِ وَالْيَوْمِ الآخِرِ فَلْيُكْرِمْ جَارَهُ،

one who forsakes his religion and abondons the community.

It was related by al-Bukhârî and Muslim.

ISLAMIC MANNERS

15. On the authority of Abû Huraira رضى الله عنه that the Messenger of Allah صلى الله عليه وسلم said:

Let him who believes in Allah and the Last Day, either speak good or keep silent, and let him who believes in Allah and the Last Day be generous to his neighbour, and let him who

وَمَنْ كَانَ يُؤْمِنُ بِاللهِ وَالْيَوْمِ الآخِرِ فَلْيُكْرِمْ ضَيْفَهُ» رَوَاهُ البُخَارِيُّ وَمُسْلِمٌ.

النهي عن الغضب

١٦ ــ عن أبي هُرَيْرَةَ رضي الله عنه، أنَّ رَجُلاً قال للنَّبِيِّ ﷺ: أَوْصِنِي قال: «لا تَغْضَبْ» فَرَدَّدَ مِرَاراً قال: «لا تَغْضَبْ» رَوَاهُ البُخَارِيُّ.

believes in Allah and the Last Day be generous to his guest.

It was related by al-Bukhârî and Muslim.

FORBIDDING OF ANGER

16. On the authority of Abû Huraira رضى الله عنه who said:

A man said to the Prophet صلى الله عليه وسلم: Counsel me. He said: Do not become angry. The man repeated [his request] several times, and he said: Do not become angry.

It was related by al-Bukhârî.

الأمر بإحسان الذبح والقتل

١٧ - عن أبي يَعْلَى شَدَّادِ بْنِ أَوْسٍ رضي الله عنه، عن رسولِ الله ﷺ، قال: «إنَّ الله كَتَبَ الإِحْسَانَ على كلِّ شيءٍ، فإذا قَتَلْتُمْ فأحْسِنُوا الْقِتْلَةَ، وإذا ذَبَحْتُمْ فأحْسِنُوا الذَّبْحَةَ، ولْيُحِدَّ أحَدُكُم شَفْرَتَه ولْيُرِحْ ذَبِيحَتَهُ» رواهُ مُسْلِمٌ.

PROFICIENCY IN ALL THINGS

17. On the authority of Abû Ya'lâ Shaddâd ibn Aus رضى الله عنه that the Messenger of Allah صلى الله عليه وسلم said:

Verily Allah has prescribed proficiency in all things. Thus, if you kill, kill well; and if you slaughter, slaughter well. Let each one of you sharpen his blade, and let him spare suffering to the animal he slaughters.

It was related by Muslim.

حسن الخلق

١٨ ــ عن أبي ذرٍّ جُنْـدُب بنِ جُنادةَ، وأبي عَبْدِ الرَّحمن مُعَاذِ بنِ جَبَلٍ رضي الله عنهما، عن رسول الله ﷺ قال: «اتَّقِ اللهَ حَيْثُمَا كُنْتَ. وأَتْبِـعِ السَّيِّئَةَ الحَسَنَةَ تَمْحُهَا، وخَالِقِ النَّاسَ بخُلُقٍ حَسَنٍ» رواهُ التِّرمذيُّ وقال حديثٌ حَسَنٌ. وفي بعضِ النُّسَخِ : حسنٌ صَحيحٌ.

GOOD BEHAVING

18.   On the authority of Abû Dharr
Jundub ibn Junâda and Abû 'Abd
ar-Rahmân Mu'âdh ibn Jabal رضى
الله عنهما that the Messenger of Allah
صلى الله عليه وسلم said:

Fear Allah wherever you are,
and follow up a bad deed with a
good one and it will wipe it out,
and behave well towards
people.

It was related by at-Tirmidhî, who
said, it is a *Hasan* (fair) *Hadith*,
and in some copies [of at-
Tirmidhî's collection] it is said to
be a *Hasan* (fair) and *Sahih*
(sound) *Hadith*.

احفظ الله يحفظك

١٩ ـ عن أبي العَبَّاس عَبْدِ الله بن عَبَّاس رضي الله عنهُمَا، قال: «كُنْتُ خَلْفَ النَّبيِّ ﷺ يوماً، فقال: يا غُلامُ إنِّي أعَلِّمُكَ كَلِماتٍ: احْفَظِ اللهَ يَحْفَظْكَ، احْفَظِ اللهَ تَجِدْهُ تُجَاهَكَ، إذا سَألْتَ فاسْألِ اللهَ، وإذا اسْتَعَنْتَ فاسْتَعِنْ بالله، واعْلَمْ أنَّ الأُمَّةَ لَو

ALWAYS REMEMBER ALLAH

19. On the authority of Abû 'Abbâs 'Abdullah, the son of 'Abbâs رضي الله عنهما, who said:

One day I was behind the Prophet صلى الله عليه وسلم and he said to me: O young man, I shall teach you some words [of advice]: Be mindful of Allah, and Allah will protect you. Be mindful of Allah, and you will find Him in front of you. If you ask, ask of Allah; if you seek help, seek help of Allah. Know that if the *Ummah* (nation, group likewise) were to gather

اجْتَمَعَتْ على أنْ يَنْفَعُوكَ بِشيءٍ لَمْ
يَنْفَعُوكَ إلّا بِشيءٍ قَدْ كَتَبَهُ الله لَكَ،
وإنِ اجْتَمَعُوا على أن يَضُرُّوكَ بِشيءٍ
لَمْ يَضُرُّوكَ إلّا بِشيءٍ قَدْ كَتَبَهُ الله
عليكَ، رُفِعَتِ الأَقْلَامُ وجَفَّتِ
الصُّحُفُ» رواهُ التِّرمـذيُّ وقالَ:
حديثٌ حسنٌ صحيحٌ، وفي روايَةٍ
غَيرِ التِّرمـذيِّ «احْفَظِ الله تَجِدْهُ
أمامَكَ، تَعَرَّفْ الى الله في الرَّخاءِ

together to benefit you with anything, it would benefit you only with something that Allah had already prescribed for you, and that if they gather together to harm you with anything, they would harm you only with something Allah had already prescribed for you. The pens have been lifted and the pages have dried[1].

It was related by at-Tirmidhî, who said it was a *Hasan* (fair) and *Sahih* (sound) *Hadith*.

---

[1] i.e. what has been written and decreed cannot be altered.

يَعرفك في الشِّدة، واعْلَمْ أنَّ ما
أخْـطَأَكَ لَمْ يَكُنْ لِيُصِيبَكَ. وما
أصابَكَ لَمْ يَكُنْ لِيُخْطِئَكَ. واعْلَمْ
أنَّ النَّصْرَ مَعَ الصَّبْر، وأنَّ الفَرَج مَعَ
الكَرْب، وأنَّ مَعَ العُسْرِ يُسْراً».

الحياء من الإيمان

٢٠ ـ   عن أبي مَسْعُودٍ عُقْبَةَ بن
عَمْرو الأنصاريِّ البَدريِّ ـ رضي

In a version other than that of at-Tirmidhî it reads:

Be mindful of Allah, you will find Him before you. Get to know Allah in prosperity and He will know you in adversity. Know that what has passed you by, was not going to befall you and that what has befallen you was not going to pass you by. And know that help comes with patience, relief with affliction, and ease with hardship.

SHAME IS PART OF *IMAN* (BELIEF)

20. On the authority of Abû Mas‘ûd, ‘Uqba ibn ‘Amr al-Ansârî al-Badrî رضى الله عنه (the one who

الله عنه ـ قال : قال رسول الله ﷺ :

«إِنَّ مِمَّا أَدْرَكَ النَّاسُ مِنْ كلامِ النُّبُوَّةِ الأولى إذا لَمْ تَسْتَحِ فاصنَعْ ما شِئْتَ» رواهُ البُخاريُّ .

قل آمنت بالله ثم استقم

٢١ ـ   عَنْ أبي عَمْرو ـ وقِيلَ أبي عَمْرة ـ سُفْيان بن عَبْدِ الله رضي الله

participated in Badr war) said: The Messenger of Allah صلى الله عليه وسلم said:

Among the words people obtained from the first prophecy[1] are: If you feel no shame, then do as you wish.

It was related by al-Bukhârî.

BELIEF IN ALLAH AND REMAINING STEADFAST ON IT

21. On the authority of Abû 'Amr — and he is also given as Abû

---

[1] i.e. those Prophets preceded our Prophet Muhammad صلى الله عليه وسلم

عنه . قال قُلْتُ : يا رسولَ الله . قُلْ
لِي في الإسلام قَوْلاً لا أَسْأَلُ عنه
أحداً غَيْرَكَ . قالَ : «قُلْ آمَنْتُ باللهِ
ثُمَّ اسْتَقِمْ» رواهُ مُسْلِمٌ .

الاقتصار على الفرائض يدخل الجنة

٢٢ ـ عن أبي عَبْدِ الله جابِرِ بن
عَبْدِ الله الأنْصَارِيِّ رضي الله
عنهُمَا : «أَنَّ رَجُلاً سَأَلَ رسولَ الله
ﷺ فقـالَ : أَرَأَيْتَ إذا صلَّيْتُ

'Amra — Sufyân ibn 'Abdullah رضى الله عنه who said:

I said: O Messenger of Allah, tell me something about Islam which I can ask of no one but you. He said: Say: I believe in Allah — and thereafter be upright.

It was related by Muslim.

DEPENDING ON OBLIGATORY DEEDS

22. On the authority of Abû 'Abdullah Jâbir, the son of 'Abdullah al-Ansârî رضى الله عنهما:

A man asked the Messenger of Allah صلى الله عليه وسلم: Do you

المَكْتُوبَاتِ، وصُمْتُ رَمَضَانَ، وأَحْلَلْتُ الحَلالَ، وحَرَّمْتُ الحَرَامَ، ولَمْ أَزِدْ على ذلك شيئاً، أَأَدْخُلُ الجَنَّةَ؟ قال: نَعَمْ» رواهُ مُسْلِمٌ.

ومَعْنى حَرَّمْتُ الحَرَامَ: اجْتَنَبْتُهُ، ومَعْنى أَحْلَلْتُ الحَلالَ: فَعَلْتُهُ مُعْتَقِداً حِلَّهُ.

الإسراع في الخير

٢٣ ـ عَنْ أَبِي مَالِكٍ الحَارِثِ بن عَاصِمٍ الأَشْعَرِيّ

think that if I perform the obligatory prayers, fast in Ramadân, treat as lawful that which is lawful and treat as forbidden that which is forbidden, and do nothing further, I shall enter Paradise? He said: Yes.

It was related by Muslim.

A GUIDE-LINE FOR A MUSLIM

23. On the authority of Abû Mâlik al-Hârith ibn 'Asim al-Ash'arî رضي الله عنه who said: The Messenger of Allah صلى الله عليه وسلم said:

Purity is half of faith. *Al-hamdulillâh* [all praise be to

رضي الله عنهُ، قال : قال رسول الله ﷺ:«الطُّهُورُ شَطْرُ الإيمانِ، والحَمْدُ لله تَمْــلأُ المِيزانَ، وسُبْحَـــانَ الله والحمدُ لله تَمْلآنِ ـ أو تَمْلأُ ـ ما بَيْنَ السَّماءِ والأرضِ ، والصَّلاةُ نُورٌ، والصَّدَقَةُ بُرْهانٌ، والصَّبْرُ ضِياءٌ، والقُرآنُ حُجَّةٌ لَكَ أو عَلَيْكَ . كُلُّ النَّاسِ يَغْدُو فَبائِعٌ نَفْسَهُ فَمُعْتِقُها أو مُوبِقُهَا» رواه مُسْلِمٌ .

Allah] fills the scale. And *Subhânallâh* [glory be to Allah and how far is He from every imperfection] and *Al-hamdulillâh* [all praise be to Allah] fill that which is between heaven and earth. Prayer is light; charity is a proof; patience is illumination; and the Qur'ân is an argument for or against you. Everyone starts his day and is vendor of his soul, either freeing it or bringing about its ruin.

It was related by Muslim.

تحريم الظلم

٢٤ ـ عَنْ أبي ذَرٍّ الغِفارِيِّ رضي الله عنه، عن النبي ﷺ فيما يَرْويه عَنْ رَبِّهِ عَزَّ وجَلَّ أنَّهُ قال: «يا عِبادي، إنِّي حَرَّمْتُ الظُّلَمَ على

FORBIDDING OF OPPRESSION

24. On the authority of Abû Dharr al-Ghifârî رضى الله عنه from the Prophet صلى الله عليه وسلم is that among the sayings[1] he relates from his *Rubb*[2] تعالى is that He said:

---

[1] i.e. in *Hadith Qudsi* (sacred *Hadith*). It means that *Hadith* in which the Prophet صلى الله عليه وسلم reports what has been revealed to him by Allah, though not necessarily in His own words. It is not a part of Qur'ân.

[2] See Foot Note on Page 19.

نَفْسِي، وَجَعَلْتُهُ بَيْنَكُمْ مُحَرَّماً، فلا تَظالَمُوا. يا عِبادِي كُلُّكُمْ ضالٌّ إلا مَنْ هَدَيْتُهُ فاسْتَهْدُونِي أَهْدِكُمْ. يا عِبادِي، كُلُّكُمْ جائِعٌ إلّا مَنْ أَطْعَمْتُهُ، فاسْتَطْعِمُونِي أُطْعِمكُمْ. يا عِبادِي، كُلُّكُمْ عارٍ إلّا مَنْ كَسَوْتُهُ، فاسْتكسوني أكْسُكُمْ. يا عِبادِي، إنَّكُمْ تُخْطِئُونَ بِاللَّيلِ والنَّهارِ وأنا أغْفِرُ الذُّنوبَ جميعاً، فاسْتَغْفِرُونِي أغْفِرْ لكُمْ. يا عِبادِي،

O My slaves, I have forbidden oppression for Myself and have made it forbidden amongst you, so do not oppress one another.

O My slaves, all of you are astray except for those I have guided, so seek guidance of Me and I shall guide you. O My slaves, all of you are hungry except for those I have fed, so seek food of Me and I shall feed you. O My slaves, all of you are naked except for those I have clothed, so seek clothing of Me and I shall clothe you. O My slaves, you commit sin by night and by day, and I forgive all sins, so seek forgiveness of Me and I shall forgive you.

إنَّكُمْ لَنْ تَبْلُغُوا ضَرِّي فَتَضُرُّونِي ،
ولَنْ تَبْلُغُوا نَفْعِي فَتَنْفَعُونِي . يَا
عِبَادِي ، لَوْ أَنَّ أَوَّلَكُمْ وَآخِرَكُمْ
وإِنْسَكُمْ وَجِنَّكُمْ كَانُوا عَلَى أَتْقَى
قَلْبِ رَجُلٍ وَاحِدٍ مِنْكُمْ مَا زَادَ ذَلِك
فِي مُلْكِي شَيْئاً . يَا عِبَادِي ، لَوْ أَنَّ
أَوَّلَكُمْ وَآخِرَكُمْ وإِنْسَكُمْ وَجِنَّكُمْ
كَانُوا عَلَى أَفْجَرِ قَلْبِ رَجُلٍ وَاحِدٍ
مِنْكُمْ مَا نَقَصَ ذَلِـكَ مِنْ مُلْكِي
شَيْئاً . يَا عِبَادِي ، لَوْ أَنَّ أَوَّلَكُمْ

O My slaves, you will not attain harming Me so as to harm Me, and you will not attain benefitting Me so as to benefit Me. O My slaves, were the first of you and the last of you, the human of you and the jinn of you to be as pious as the most pious heart of anyone man of you, that would not increase My kingdom in anything. O My slaves, were the first of you and the last of you, the human of you and the jinn of you to be as wicked as the most wicked heart of any one man of you, that would not decrease My kingdom in anything. O My slaves, were the first of you and

وآخرَكُمْ وإنْسَكُمْ وجِنَّكُمْ قامُوا في
صَعِيدٍ واحِدٍ فَسَألُوني فَأعْطَيْتُ كلَّ
واحِدٍ مَسْألَتَهُ ما نَقَصَ ذلِك مِمَّا
عِنْدي إلا كما يَنْقُصُ المِخْيَطُ إذا
أُدْخِلَ البَحْرَ. يا عِبادي، إنَّما هِيَ
أعْمالُكُمْ أُحْصِيها لَكُمْ ثُمَّ أُوَفِّيكُمْ
إيّاها. فَمَنْ وَجَدَ خيراً فَلْيَحْمَدِ الله،
ومَنْ وَجَدَ غَيْرَ ذلِك فلا يَلُومَنَّ إلّا
نَفْسَهُ» رواهُ مُسْلم.

the last of you, the human of you and the jinn of you to rise up in one place and make a request of Me, and were I to give everyone what he requested, that would not decrease what I have, any more than a needle decreases the sea if put into it.

O My slaves, it is but your deeds that I reckon up for you and then recompense you for, so let him who finds good, praise Allah and let him who finds other than that, blame no one but himself.

It was related by Muslim.

ذهب أهل الدثور بالأجور

٢٥ ـ عن أبي ذرٍ رضي الله عنه أيضاً: «أنَّ ناساً من أصحاب رسولِ اللهِ ﷺ قالوا للنبيِّ ﷺ يا رسولَ الله، ذهبَ أهْلُ الدُّثورِ بالأجورِ يُصَلُّونَ كما نُصَلِّي، ويَصُومُونَ كما نَصُومُ ويَتَصَدَّقُونَ بفُضُولِ أمْوالِهم .. قال: أوَ لَيْسَ قَدْ جَعَلَ اللهُ لَكُمْ ما تَصَدَّقُونَ: إنَّ

ALL ACTIONS OF A BELIEVER ARE CHARITY

25. Also on the authority of Abû Dharr رضى الله عنه :

Some of the companions of the Messenger of Allah صلى الله عليه وسلم said to the Prophet صلى الله عليه وسلم: O Messenger of Allah, the affluent have made off with the rewards: they pray as we pray, they fast as we fast, and they give away in charity the superfluity of their wealth.

He said: Has not Allah made things for you to give away in charity? Truly every *tasbîh*[1] is a

---

[1] To say: *Subhanallah* (glory be to Allah).

لكُمْ بكُلِّ تَسْبِيحَةٍ صَدَقَةً، وكلِّ
تَكْبِيرَةٍ صَدَقَـةً، وكلِّ تَحْمِيدةٍ
صَدَقَةً، وكلِّ تَهْلِيلةٍ صَدَقَةً، وأمْرٍ
بالمَعْرُوفِ صَدَقَة، ونهيٍ عن مُنْكَرٍ
صَدَقَةً، وفي بُضْعِ أحَدِكُمْ صَدَقَةً.
قالُـوا: يا رسولَ الله، أيأتي أحَدُنا
شَهْـوَتَهُ ويكُونُ لهُ فيها أجرٌ؟ قال

charity, every *takbîr*[1] is a charity, every *tahmîd*[2] is a charity, and every *tahlîl*[3] is a charity; to enjoin a good action is a charity, to forbid an evil action is a charity, and in the sexual act of each of you there is a charity.

They said: O Messenger of Allah صلى الله عليه وسلم , when one of us fulfils his sexual desire will have some reward for that?

---

[1] To say *Allahu Akbar* (Allah is most Great).

[2] To say *Alhamdu lillah* (all praise be to Allah).

[3] To say *la ilaha ill-Allah* i.e. there is no god to be worshipped but Allah.

أَرَأَيْتُمْ لَوْ وَضَعَهَا فِي حَرَامٍ أَكَانَ عَلَيْهِ وِزْرٌ؟ فَكَذَلِكَ إِذَا وَضَعَهَا فِي الْحَلَالِ كَانَ لَهُ أَجْرٌ» رَوَاهُ مُسْلِمٌ.

فضـل الإصـلاح بين النـاس والعدل بينهم وإعانتهم

٢٦ - عن أبي هُرَيْرَةَ رضي الله عنه قال: قال رسولُ الله ﷺ «كُلُّ سُلَامَى مِنَ النَّاسِ عليه صَدَقَةٌ. كل يَوْمٍ تَطْلُعُ فِيهِ الشَّمْسُ: تَعْدِلُ

He said: Do you [not] think that were he to act upon it unlawfully he would be sinning? Likewise, if he has acted upon it lawfully he will have a reward.

It was related by Muslim.

MINOR ACTS ARE VALUABLE

26. On the authority of Abû Huraira رضى الله عنه who said: The Messenger of Allah صلى الله عليه وسلم said:

Each person's every joint must do a charity every day the sun comes up: to act justly between

بَيْنَ اثْنَيْنِ صَدَقَةٌ. وتُعينُ الرَّجُلَ في دَابَّتِه فَتَحْمِلُهُ عليها أو تَرْفَعُ لهُ عليها مَتَاعَهُ صَدَقَةٌ، والكلمةُ الطَّيبةُ صَدَقَةٌ، وبكلِّ خُطوةٍ تَمشيها الى الصَّلاةِ صَدَقَةٌ، وتُميطُ الأذى عنِ الطَّريقِ صَدَقَةٌ» رواهُ البُخاري ومُسْلِمٌ.

البر حسن الخلق

٢٧ - عن النَّوَّاسِ بنِ سَمْعَانَ رضي الله عنه، عن النبي ﷺ قال:

two people is a charity; to help a man with his mount, lifting him onto it or hoisting up his belongings onto it is a charity; a good word is a charity; every step you take to perform prayers is a charity; and removing a harmful thing from the road is a charity.

It was related by al-Bukhârî and Muslim.

DEFINITION OF RIGHTEOUSNESS

27. On the authority of an-Nawwâs ibn Sam'ân رضى الله عنه that the Prophet صلى الله عليه وسلم said:

«الْبِرُّ حُسْنُ الخُلُقِ والإِثْمُ ما حاكَ في نَفْسِكَ وكَرِهْتَ أنْ يَطَّلِعَ عليه النَّاسُ» رواهُ مُسْلِمٌ وعن وابِصَةَ بنِ مَعْبَدٍ رضي الله عنه قال: أَتَيْتُ رسولَ اللهِ ﷺ فقالَ: جِئْتَ تَسْأَلُ عن البِرِّ؟ قُلْتُ: نعمْ. قال: «اسْتَفْتِ قَلْبَكَ، البِرُّ ما اطْمَأَنَّتْ إليه النَّفْسُ واطْمَأَنَّ إليه القَلْبُ، والإِثْمُ ما حاكَ في النَّفْسِ وتَرَدَّدَ في

Righteousness is good morality, and wrongdoing is that which wavers in your heart and which you dislike people finding out about.

It was related by Muslim

On the authority of Wâbisa ibn Ma'bad رضى الله عنه who said:

I came to the Messenger of Allah صلى الله عليه وسلم and he said: You have come to ask about righteousness? I said: Yes. He said: Consult your heart. Righteousness is that about which the soul feels tranquil and the heart feels tranquil, and wrongdoing is that which wavers in the soul and moves to

الصَّدْر، وإنْ أَفْتَاكَ النَّاسُ وأَفْتُوكَ»

حديث حَسَنٌ رَوَيْنَاهُ في مُسْنَدَي

الإِمَامَيْنِ أحمدَ بنِ حَنْبَلٍ والدَّارمي

بإسنادٍ حَسَنٍ .

وجوب لزوم السنة

٢٨ ـ عـن أبـي نَجِيـحٍ

الْعِرباضِ بنِ ساريةَ رضي الله عنه

قال «وعَـظَنَا رسولُ الله ﷺ مَوْعِظَةً

and fro in the breast even though people again and again have given you their legal opinion [in its favour].

A *Hasan* (fair) *Hadith* which we have transmitted from the two *Imâms*, Ahmad ibn Hanbal and ad-Dârimî, with a *Hasan* (fair) chain of authority.

MUST KEEP TO THE PROPHET'S *SUNNA*

28. On the authority of Abû Najîh al-'Irbâd ibn Sâriya رضى الله عنه who said:

The Messenger of Allah صلى الله عليه وسلم gave us a sermon by which our hearts were filled

وَجِلَتْ مِنْها القُلُوبُ، وذَرِفَتْ مِنْها
العُيُونُ فَقُلْنَا: يا رسولَ الله، كأنَّها
مَوْعِظَةُ مُوَدِّعٍ فأَوْصِنَا. قال:
أُوصِيكُمْ بِتَقْوَى الله عزَّ وَجَلَّ،
والسَّمعِ والطَّاعَةِ، وإِنْ تَأَمَّرَ عَلَيْكُمْ
عَبْدٌ، فإِنَّهُ مَنْ يَعِشْ مِنْكُمْ فَسَيَرَى
اخْتِلافاً كثيراً. فَعَلَيكُمْ بِسُنَّتِي وسُنَّةِ

with fear and tears came to our eyes. We said: O Messenger of Allah, it is as though this a farewell sermon, so counsel us. He said: I counsel you to fear Allah عزوجل and to give absolute obedience even if a slave becomes your leader. Verily he among you who lives [long] will see great controversy, so you must keep to my *sunna*[1] and to the *sunna*

---

[1] The original meaning of the word *sunna* is "Way or Path" to be followed, but it is used as a technical term (i.e. in religious terms) for those words, deeds, and sanctions of the Prophet صلى الله عليه وسلم =

الخُلَفَاءِ الرَّاشِدِينَ المَهْدِيِّينَ، عَضُّوا عَلَيْهَا بِالنَّوَاجِذِ، و إِيَّاكُمْ و مُحْدَثَاتِ الأُمُورِ، فَإِنَّ كُلَّ مُحْدَثَةٍ بِدْعَـةٌ، و كُلَّ بِدْعَةٍ ضَلَالَةٌ». رواهُ أبوداود

of the rightly-guided Rashidite Caliphs[1] — cling to them stubbornly. Beware of newly invented matters, for every invented matter is an innovation and every innovation is a going

---

= that were reported and have come down to us. It is obligatory for each one to follow the Prophet's *sunna* in all aspect of the life.

[1] This is the title of the first four Islami Caliphs (i.e. Abu Bakr, Umar, Uthman and Ali رضى الله عنهم) and is generally rendered as orthodox caliphs, that is not good. So it is better to be written in the same word and explained as the rightly guided ones.

و الترمـذيُّ و قـال حديثٌ حسنٌ
صحيحٌ .

ما يدخل الجنة

٢٩ ـ   عن مُعاذِ بن جَبَلٍ رضي
الله عنه ، قال : قُلْتُ يا رسولَ الله ،
أخبِـرْني بعَمَـلٍ يُدخِلُني الجنَّـةَ
ويُبـاعِدُني عن النَّارِ ، قال : لَقَـدْ
سألتَ عن عظيمٍ ، وإنَّهُ لَيَسيرٌ على

astray.

It was related by Abû Dâwûd and at-Tirmidhî, who stated it as a *Hasan* (fair) and *Sahih* (sound) *Hadith*.

WHAT DEEDS ADMIT YOU IN PARADISE

29. On the authority of Mu'adh ibn Jabal رضى الله عنه who said:

I said: O Messenger of Allah, tell me of an act which will take me into the Paradise and will keep me away from the Hell-fire. He said: You have asked me about a major matter, yet it is easy for him for whom Allah the Exalted makes it

مَنْ يَسَّرَهُ الله تعالى عليه : تَعْبُدُ الله
لا تُشْرِكُ به شيئاً، وتُقيمُ الصَّلاةَ،
وتُؤْتِي الزَّكاةَ، وتصُومُ رَمَضانَ وتحجُّ
البَيْتَ ، ثُمَّ قال : ألا أَدُلُّكَ على
أَبْـوابِ الْخَيْرِ؟ الصَّوْمُ جُنَّـةٌ ،
والصَّدَقَة تُطْفِئ الْخَطِيئَة كما
يُطْفِئُ الْماءُ النَّارَ، وصَلاةُ الرَّجُلِ
في جَوْفِ اللَّيْلِ . ثُمَّ تَلا ﴿تَتَجافَى
جُنوبُهُمْ عَنِ المَضاجِعِ﴾ . حتى

easy. You should worship Allah, associating nothing with Him; you should perform the prayers; you should pay the *zakat,* you should fast in Ramdân; and you should make the pilgrimage to the House. Then he said: Shall I not show you the gates of goodness? Fasting [which] is a shield; charity extinguishes sin as water extinguishes fire; and the praying of a man in the depths of night. Then he recited: "Their sides forsake their beds invoking their *Rubb*[1] in fear and hope and they spend out of what we have bestowed on them. No person

---

[1] See foot note on page 19.

بَلَغَ ﴿يَعْمَلُونَ﴾ ثُمَّ قَالَ: أَلَا أُخْبِرُكَ
بِرَأْسِ الْأَمْرِ وَعَمُودِهِ وَذِرْوَةِ سَنَامِهِ؟
قُلْتُ: بَلَى يَا رَسُولَ اللهِ، قَالَ:
رَأْسُ الْأَمْرِ الْإِسْلَامُ، وَعَمُودُهُ
الصَّلَاةُ، وَذِرْوَةُ سَنَامِهِ الْجِهَادُ. ثُمَّ
قَالَ: أَلَا أُخْبِرُكَ بِمِلَاكِ ذَلِكَ كُلِّهِ؟
فَقُلْتُ: بَلَى يَا رَسُولَ اللهِ، فَأَخَذَ
بِلِسَانِهِ وَقَالَ: كُفَّ عَلَيْكَ هَذَا.
قُلْتُ: يَا نَبِيَّ اللهِ، وَإِنَّا لَمُؤَاخَذُونَ
بِمَا نَتَكَلَّمُ بِهِ؟ فَقَالَ: ثَكِلَتْكَ أُمُّكَ،

knows what is kept hidden for them of joy as a reward for what they used to do[1] ." Then he said: Shall I not tell you of the peak of the matter, its pillar, and its topmost part? I said: Yes, O Messenger of Allah. He said: The peak of the matter is Islam; the pillar is prayer; and its topmost part is *jihâd*. Then he said: Shall I not tell you of the controlling of all that? I said: Yes, O Messenger of Allah. And he took hold of his tongue and said: Restrain this. I said: O Prophet of Allah, will what we say be held against us? He said: May your mother be bereaved of

---

1. as-Sajdah, 16,17.

وهَلْ يَكُبُّ النَّاسَ في النَّارِ على وُجُوهِهِمْ ـ أو قال على مَنَاخِرِهِمْ ـ إلا حَصَائِدُ ألسِنَتِهِمْ» رواهُ التِّرْمِذِيُّ وقال: حديثٌ حَسَنٌ صَحيحٌ.

حقوق الله تعالى

٣٠ ـ عن أبي ثَعْلَبَةَ الخُشَنِيِّ ـ جُرْثُومِ بنِ ناشِرٍ ـ رضي الله عنه، عن رسولِ اللهِ ﷺ قال: «إنَّ اللهَ تعالى فَرَضَ فَرائِضَ فَلا تُضيِّعُوهَا،

you, O Mu'âdh! Is there anything that topples people on their faces – or he said on their noses – into Hell-fire other than the harvests of their tongues?

It was related by at-Tirmidhî, who stated that as a *Hasan* (fair) and *Sahih* (sound) *Hadith*.

THE LIMITS SET BY ALLAH

30. On the authority of Abû Tha'laba al-Khushanî Jurthûm ibn Nâshir رضى الله عنه that the Messenger of Allah صلى الله عليه وسلم said:

Allah, the Exalted prescribed religious duties, so do not neglect

وَحَدَّ حُدُوداً فَلَا تَعْتَدُوهَا، وحَرَّمَ
أَشْيَاءَ فَلَا تَنْتَهِكُوهَا، وسَكَتَ عن
أَشْيَاءَ رَحْمَةً لَكُمْ غَيْرَ نِسْيَانٍ فلا
تَبْحَثُوا عنها» حديثٌ حسنٌ رَوَاهُ
الدَّار قُطْنِيُّ وَغَيْرُهُ.

الزهد الحقيقي

٣١ ـ عـن أبي العَبَّاس ـ
سَهْل بن سَعْدٍ السَّاعِدِيِّ ـ رضي
الله عنه قال: «جَاءَ رَجُلٌ الى النَّبِيِّ

them; He has set boundaries, so do not over step them; He has prohibited some things, so do not violate them; about some things He was silent – out of compassion for you, not forgetfulness –, so seek not after them.

A *Hasan* (fair) *Hadith* related by ad-Dâraqutnî and other.

TRUE RENOUNCING

31. On the authority of Abû al-'Abbâs Sahl ibn Sa'd as-Sâ'idî رضى الله عنه who said:

A man came to the Prophet صلى الله عليه وسلم and said: O

فقال ﷺ: يا رسولَ اللهِ، دُلَّني على عَمَلٍ إذا عَمِلْتُهُ أَحَبَّني اللهُ وأَحَبَّني النَّاسُ، فقالَ: ازْهَدْ في الدُّنْيَا يُحِبَّكَ اللهُ، وازْهَدْ فيما عِنْدَ النَّاس يُحِبَّكَ النَّاسُ» حديثٌ حَسَنٌ رواهُ ابنُ ماجَهْ وغَيْرُهُ بأسانيدَ حَسَنَةٍ .

لا ضررَ ولا ضِرار

٣٢ ـ عن أبي سَعيدٍ ـ سَعْدِ بنِ سِنَانٍ ـ الخُدريِّ رضي الله عنه أنَّ

Messenger of Allah, direct me to an act which, if I do it, [will cause] Allah to love me and people to love me. He said: Renounce the world and Allah will love you, and renounce what people possess and people will love you.

A *Hasan* (fair) *Hadith* related by Ibn Mâjah and others with good chains of authorities.

NEITHER HARMING NOR RECIPROCATING HARM

32. On the authority of Abû Sa'îd Sa'd ibn Mâlik ibn Sinân al-Khudrî رضى الله عنه the Messenger of Allah صلى الله عليه وسلم said:

رسولَ الله ﷺ قال: «لا ضَرَرَ ولا ضِرَارَ» حديث حَسَنٌ رَواهُ ابنُ ماجَهْ والدَّارَ قُطْنِيُّ وغَيْرُهُمَا مُسْنَداً، وَرَوَاهُ مالِكُ في المُوَطَّأ مُرْسَلاً عن عَمْرِو بنِ يَحْيَى عن أبيهِ عن النَّبيِّ

There should be neither
harming nor reciprocating
harm.

A *Hasan* (fair) *Hadith* narrated by
Ibn Mâjah, ad-Dâraqutnî and
others and ranked as *musnad*[1] . It
was also narrated by Mâlik in al-
Muwatta as *mursal*[2] with a chain of
authorities from 'Amr ibn Yahyâ,
from his father, from the Prophet

---

[1] A *musnad Hadith* is one with a
complete chain of authorities from the
narrator to the Prophet himself .

[2] A *mursal* is one where the chain of
authorities ends with the follower and
does not give the name of the companion
who lies, in the chain, between the
follower and the Prophet himself. The
authenticity of a *mursal Hadith* is=

ﷺ، فَأَسْقَطَ أَبَا سَعِيدٍ وَلَهُ طُرُقٌ
يُقَوِّي بَعْضُهَا بَعْضاً.

البينـة على المدعي واليمين على من أنكر

٣٣ - عن ابن عَبَّاسٍ رضي الله
عَنْهُمَا، أَنَّ رَسُولَ اللهِ ﷺ قَالَ: «لَوْ
يُعْطَى النَّاسُ بِدَعْوَاهُمْ، لَادَّعَى
رِجَالٌ أَمْوَالَ قَوْمٍ وَدِماءَهُمْ، لَكِنِ

صلى الله عليه وسلم but leaving out Abû Sa'îd, and he has other chains of authorities that support one another.

PROOF ON CLAIMANT AND OATH UPON DENIER

33. On the authority of Ibn 'Abbâs رضى الله عنهما that the Messenger of Allah صلى الله عليه وسلم said:

> Were people to be given in accordance with their claim, men would claim the fortunes and lives of [other] people, but the onus of proof is on the

---

= strengthened if supported by another *mursal Hadith* with a different chain of authorities.

الْبَيِّنَةُ عَلَى الْمُدَّعِي وَالْيَمِينُ عَلَى مَنْ أَنْكَرَ» حديثٌ حسنٌ رَوَاهُ الْبَيْهَقِيُّ وَغَيْرُهُ هَكَذَا، وَبَعْضُهُ فِي الصَّحِيحَيْنِ .

النهي عن المنكر من الإيمان

٣٤ - عن أبي سَعِيدٍ الخُدْرِيِّ

claimant and the taking of an oath is incumbent upon him who denies.

A *Hasan* (fair) *Hadith* related by al-Baihaqî and others in this form, and part of it is in the two *Sahîhs*.

FORBIDDING THE EVIL IS PART OF *IMAN*

34. On the authority of Abû Sa'îd al-Khudrî رضى الله عنه, who said: I

رضِيَ اللهُ عنهُ قال: سَمِعْتُ رسُولَ اللهِ ﷺ يقولُ: «مَنْ رَأى مِنْكُمْ مُنْكَراً فَلْيُغَيِّرْهُ بِيَدِهِ، فإنْ لَمْ يَسْتَطِعْ فَبِلِسَانِهِ، فإنْ لَمْ يَسْتَطِعْ فَبِقَلْبِهِ وذلك أَضْعَفُ الإِيمَانِ» رواهُ مُسْلِمٌ.

heard the Messenger of Allah صلى
الله عليه وسلم saying:

Whosoever of you sees an evil[1],
let him change it with his hand;
and if he is not able to do so,
then with his tongue; and if he
is not able to do so, then with
his heart – and that is the
weakest of faith.

It was narrated by Muslim.

---

[1] Enjoining the people to do right and
forbidding them from evil is very
important in Islam. Therefore some *salaf*
(predecessor religious scholars) counted it
the sixth pillar in Islâm.

أخوة الإسلام

٣٥ ـ عن أبي هُرَيْرَةَ رضي الله
عنه ، قال : قال رَسُولُ الله ﷺ : «لا
تَحَاسَدُوا، ولا تَنَاجَشُوا، ولا
تَبَاغَضُوا، ولا تَدَابَرُوا، ولا يَبِعْ
بَعْضُكُم على بَيْع بَعْض ، وكُونُوا
عِبَادَ الله إخْوَاناً. المُسْلِمُ أَخُو
المُسْلِمِ : لا يَظْلِمُهُ، ولا يَخْذُلُهُ،
ولا يَكْذِبُهُ، ولا يَحْقِرُهُ. التَّقْوَى

35. On the authority of Abû Huraira رضى الله عنه, who said: the Messenger of Allah صلى الله عليه وسلم said:

Do not envy one another; do not inflate prices one to another; do not hate one another; do not turn away from one another; and do not undercut one another, but be you, O slaves of Allah, brothers. A Muslim is the brother of a Muslim: he neither oppresses him nor disgraces him, he neither lies to him nor does he hold him in contempt.

هَهُنَا ـ وَيُشِيرُ الى صَدْرِه ثَلَاث مَرَّاتٍ ـ بِحَسْبِ امْرِىءٍ مِنَ الشَّرِّ أنْ يَحْقِرَ أخاهُ المُسْلِمَ، كُلُّ المُسْلِمِ على المُسْلِمِ حَرَامٌ: دَمُهُ وَمالُهُ وَعِرْضُهُ» رَواهُ مُسْلِمٌ.

فضـل الاجتمـاع على تلاوة القرآن وعلى الذكر

٣٦ ـ عن أبي هُرَيْرَةَ رضي الله عنه، عن النَّبِيِّ ﷺ قال: «مَنْ نَفَّسَ

Piety and righteousness is here – and he pointed to his breast three times. It is evil enough for a man to hold his brother Muslim in contempt. The whole of a Muslim for another Muslim is inviolable: his blood, his property, and his honour.

It was related by Muslim.

ALLAH HELPS THOSE WHO HELP OTHERS

36. On the authority of Abû Huraira رضى الله عنه that the Prophet صلى الله عليه وسلم said:

Whosoever removes a worldly grief from a believer, Allah will

عن مُؤمِنٍ كُربةً من كُرب الـدُّنْيا
نَفَّسَ الله عَنْهُ كُرْبةً من كُرَبِ يومِ
القِيامَةِ، ومَنْ يَسَّرَ على مُعْسِرٍ يَسَّرَ
الله عليهِ في الـدُّنْيا والآخِرةِ، ومَنْ
سَتَرَ مُسْلِماً سَتَرَهُ الله في الـدُّنْيا
والآخِرةِ، والله في عَوْنِ الـعَبْدِ ما
كانَ الـعَبْدُ في عَوْنِ أخيهِ. ومَنْ
سَلَكَ طَريقاً يَلْتَمِسُ فيهِ عِلْماً سَهَّلَ
الله به طَريقاً الى الجنَّةِ، وما اجْتَمَعَ
قومٌ في بَيْتٍ من بُيُوتِ الله يتْـلُونَ
كِتَابَ الله ويَتَدَارَسُونَهُ بَيْنَهُمْ إلاَّ نَزَلَتْ

remove from him one of the griefs of the Day of Judgment. Whosoever alleviates [the lot of] a needy person, Allah will alleviate [his lot] in this world and the next. Whosoever shields a Muslims, Allah will shield him in this world and the next. Allah will aid a slave [of His] so long as the slave aids his brother. Whosoever follows a path to seek knowledge therein, Allah will make easy for him a path to Paradise. No people gather together in one of the houses of Allah, reciting the Book of Allah and studying it among themselves, but tranquillity and peace descends

عليهم السَّكِينَةُ، وغَشِيتهُمُ الرَّحْمَةُ، وحَفَّتهُمُ المَلائِكَةُ، وذَكَرَهُمُ اللهُ فيمَنْ عِنْدَه، وَمَنْ بطَّأ به عَمَلُهُ لَمْ يُسْرِعْ به نَسَبُهُ» رواهُ مُسْلِمٌ بهذا اللفظِ .

فضل الله تعالى ورحمته

٣٧ ـ   عن ابنِ عبّاسٍ رِضِي اللهُ عنهُمَا. عن رسولِ اللهِ ﷺ فيما يَرْوِيهِ عن ربِّهِ تَبارَكَ وتعالى قال :

upon them, mercy envelopes them, the angels surround them Allah makes mention of them amongst those who are with Him. And whosoever is slowed down by his actions will not be hastened forward by his lineage.

It was related by Muslim in these words.

THE COMPASSION OF ALLAH UPON HIS SLAVES

37. On the authority of the Ibn 'Abbâs رضى الله عنهما, from the Messenger of Allah صلى الله عليه وسلم is that among the sayings he relates from his Lord (Glorified and Exalted be He) is that he said:

«إنَّ اللهَ كَتَبَ الحَسَنَاتِ والسَّيِّئَاتِ،
ثُمَّ بَيَّنَ ذلك: فَمَنْ هَمَّ بِحَسَنَةٍ فَلَمْ
يَعْمَلْها كَتَبَها اللهُ عِنْدَهُ حَسَنَةً كامِلَةً،
وإنْ هَمَّ بها فَعَمِلَها كَتَبَها اللهُ عِنْدَهُ
عَشْرَ حَسَنَاتٍ الى سَبْعِمائَةِ ضِعْفٍ
الى أَضْعَافٍ كَثِيرَةٍ، وإنْ هَمَّ بِسَيِّئَةٍ
فَلَمْ يَعْمَلْها كَتَبَها اللهُ عِنْدَهُ حَسَنَةً
كامِلَةً، وإنْ هَمَّ بها فَعَمِلَها كَتَبَها
اللهُ سَيِّئَةً واحِدَةً» رواهُ البُخارِيُّ

Allah has written down the good deeds and the bad ones. Then He explained it [by saying that] he who has intended a good deed and has not done it, Allah writes it down with Himself as a full good deed, but if he has intended it and has done it, Allah writes it down with Himself as from ten good deeds to seven hundred times, or many times over. But if he has intended a bad deed and has not done it, Allah writes it down with Himself as a full good deed, but if he has intended it and has done it, Allah writes it down as one bad deed.

ومُسْلِمٌ في صَحِيحَيْهِما بهذه الحُرُوفِ.

العبادة لله وسيلة القرب والمحبة

٣٨ ـ عن أبي هُرَيْرَةَ رضي الله عنه قال: قال رسولُ الله ﷺ: إنَّ الله تعالى قال: «مَنْ عادَى لي وَلِيًّا فَقَدْ آذَنْتُهُ بِالحَرْبِ، وما تَقَرَّبَ إليَّ عَبْدِي بِشَيءٍ أُحبَّ إليَّ مِمَّا افْتَرَضْتُهُ

It was related by al-Bukhârî and Muslim in their two *Sahîhs* in these words.

APPROACH ALLAH WITH *NAWAFIL*

38. On the authority of Abû Huraira رضى الله عنه who said: the Messenger of Allah صلى الله عليه وسلم said:

Allah, the Exalted has said: Whosoever shows enmity to a friend of Mine, I shall be at war with him. My slave does not draw near to Me with anything more loved by Me than the religious duties I have imposed upon him, and My slave

عليه ، ولا يَزَالُ عَبْدِي يَتَقَرَّبُ إليَّ
بالنَّوَافِل حتى أحِبَّهُ ، فإذا أحْبَبْتُهُ
كُنْتُ سَمْعَهُ الذي يَسْمَعُ به ، وبَصَرُهُ
الَّذِي يُبْصِرُ به ، وَيَدَهُ التي يَبْطِشُ
بها ، ورجْلَهُ التي يَمْشِي بها ، ولَئِنْ
سَأَلَنِي لأعْطِيَنَّهُ ، ولَئِن اسْتَعَاذَنِي
لأعِيذَنَّهُ» رواهُ البُخَارِيُّ .

continues to draw near to Me with supererogatory works so that I shall love him. When I love him I am his hearing[1] with which he hears, his seeing with which he sees, his hand with which he holds, and his foot with which he walks. Were he to ask [something] of Me, I would surely give it to him; and were he to ask Me for refuge, I would surely grant him it.

It was related by al-Bukhârî.

---

[1] What is named and qualified for Allah by Himself or His Messenger, we confirm them and believe in completely without changing or ignoring them or twisting the

التجاوز عن المخطىء والناسي والمكره

٣٩ ـ عن ابن عَبَّاسٍ رضي الله عنهما: أن رسولَ الله ﷺ قال: «إنَّ الله تَجَاوَزَ لِي عن أمَّتي: الخَطَأ، والنِّسْيَانَ، ومـا اسْتُكْرِهُوا عليه» حديثٌ حسـنٌ رواهُ ابـنُ ماجَـه والْبَيْهَقيُّ. وغيْرُهُما.

PARDONING OF MISTAKES AND FORGETFULNESS

39. On the authority of Ibn 'Abbâs رضى الله عنهما that the Messenger of Allah صلى الله عليه وسلم said:

Allah has pardoned for me my people for [their] mistakes and [their] forgetfulness and for what they have done under duress.

---

meaning or giving resemblance to others just as in the above *Hadith*, there is hearing, seeing, hand and foot for Allah, so we believe in all them and confirm them without similarity or twisting the meaning for them.

الدنيا وسيلة ومزرعة للآخرة

٤٠ ـ عن ابن عُمَر رضي الله عنهما قال: «أخَذَ رسولُ الله ﷺ بِمَنْكِبَيَّ فقال: كُنْ في الدُّنيا كأنَّك غريبٌ أو عابرُ سبيل» وكان ابنُ عمرَ رضي الله عنهما يقولُ: «إذا أمْسَيْتَ فلا تَنْتَظِرِ الصَّباحَ، وإذا أصْبَحْتَ

A *Hasan* (fair) *Hadith* related by
Ibn Mâjah, al-Baihaqî, and others.

THE LIFE OF THIS WORLD

40. On the authority of Ibn 'Umar
رضى الله عنهما who said:

The Messenger of Allah صلى الله
عليه وسلم took me by the shoulder
and said: Be in the world as
though you were a stranger or a
wayfarer.

Ibn 'Umar رضى الله عنهما used to say:

At evening do not expect [to
live till] morning, and at
morning do not expect [to live
till] evening. Take from your

فلا تَنْتَظِر المَساءَ، وخُذْ مِنْ صِحَّتِكَ لِمَرضِكَ، ومِنْ حَياتِكَ لِمَوْتِكَ». رواهُ البُخاريُّ.

علامة الإيمان

٤١ ـ عـن أبي مُحَمَّدٍ عبد الله بن عَمْروبن العَاص رضي الله عنهُمَا، قالَ: قالَ رَسُولُ الله ﷺ:

health for your illness and from
your life for your death.

It was related by al-Bukhârî.

FOLLOW-UP WHAT THE PROPHET HAS BROUGHT

41.[1] On the authority of Abû
Muhammad 'Abdullah, the son of
'Amr ibn al-'As رضى الله عنهما who
said: The Messenger of Allah صلى
الله عليه وسلم said:

---

[1] The compiler has allowed himself to
add two further *Ahadith* to the recognised
number of forty, although the title
remains *An-Nawawis Forty*.

«لَا يُؤْمِنُ أَحَدُكُمْ حَتَّى يَكُونَ هَوَاهُ تَبَعاً لِمَا جِئْتُ بِهِ» حديثٌ حسنٌ صحيحٌ، رَوَيْنَاهُ في كِتَابِ الحُجَّةِ بِإِسْنَادٍ صحيحٍ.

سعة مغفرة الله تعالى

٤٢ ـ عن أنسٍ رضي الله عنه، قال: سمعتُ رسولَ الله ﷺ يقول:

None of you [truly] be a believer until his inclination is in accordance with what I have brought.

A *Hasan* (fair) and *Sahih* (sound) *Hadith* which we have transmitted from Kitâb al-Hujja[1] with a sound chain of authorities.

ALLAH IS ALL-FORGIVING

42. On the authority of Anas رضى الله عنه who said: I heard the Messenger of Allah صلى الله عليه وسلم saying:

---

[1] The title of a book by Abul Qasim Ismail bin Muhammad al-Asfahani (died 535 H.)

«قال الله تعالى : يا ابنَ آدَمَ ، إنَّكَ ما دَعَوْتَني ورَجَوْتَني غَفَرْتُ لَكَ على ما كانَ مِنكَ ولا أُبالي ، يا ابنَ آدَمَ ، لَوْ بَلَغَتْ ذُنُوبُكَ عَنانَ السَّماءِ ثُمَّ اسْتَغْفَرْتَني غَفَرْتُ لَكَ ، يا ابنَ آدَمَ ، إنَّكَ لَوْ أَتَيْتَني بِقُرابِ الأرضِ خَطايا ثُمَّ لَقِيتَني لا تُشْرِكُ بي شَيْئاً لَأَتَيْتُكَ بِقُرابِها مَغْفِرَةً» رواهُ التِّرمِذيُّ وقال حديثٌ حسنٌ صحيحٌ .

Allah, the Exalted has said: O son of Adam, so long as you call upon Me and ask of Me, I shall forgive you for what you have done, and I shall not mind. O son of Adam, were your sins to reach the clouds of the sky and were you then to ask forgiveness of Me, I would forgive you. O son of Adam, were you to come to Me with sins nearly as great as the earth and were you then to face Me, ascribing no partner to Me, I would bring you forgiveness nearly as great as it.

It was related by at-Tirmidhî, who stated that as a *Hasan* (fair) and *Sahih* (sound) *Hadith*.

CONTENTS